CONTENTS

creative Handcrafts

for Youth

98 Handcrafts for
Church • School • VBS • Home
8 pages of Recipes and Hints

Compiled by Eleanor L. Doan

A Division of G/L Publications
Glendale, California, U.S.A.

41
745

ACKNOWLEDGMENT
The handcrafts included in this book are taken from the *Handcraft Encyclopedia* by the same author. They are assembled here for greater convenience in use with youth.

Published by
Regal Books Division, G/L Publications
Glendale, California 91209, U.S.A.
Library of Congress Catalog No.: 72-93603
ISBN 0-8307-0211-3

HINTS

CORNER SHELF

Materials: 3 wooden boxes—11½"x11½"x8½", 10"x 10"x6½", 8½"x8½"x5½"; 4 metal or wood cleats; small nails; hammer; sandpaper; varnish; brush; 2 screw eyes; wire

Each set of three boxes will provide material for two sets of corner shelves. Fruit packing boxes with sides and ends the same thickness are suggested.

Procedure: Saw across each box diagonally, leaving two corners intact. Use boxes in graduated sizes with the largest box on the bottom. Nail cleats on upper and lower sides of back of middle-size shelf. Place on bottom shelf and nail cleats so shelves will be fastened together. (If lowest box has no bottom, cut one to fit from the end of an orange crate.) Place top shelf on middle shelf and nail cleats.

When shelves are assembled, sandpaper until smooth; then varnish or enamel. This will make a nice corner shelf for almost any room in the house. Put 2 screw eyes in back of shelves, one on each side of corner, and attach a piece of wire for a hanger.

Time required to make: 2 to 3 hours

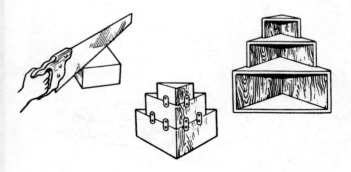

1

HASP BELT

Materials: 1 hasp; rivets; leather belt or strip of leather to fit waist and as wide as hasp; knife; pencil; awl or leather punch; hammer; small chain, plastic lacing or a lightweight padlock and key

Procedure: Cut belt exact measurement of waist. Place ends together and arrange the 2 parts of hasp in position. Mark rivet holes with pencil (sketch a). Remove hasp and punch holes for rivets. Place hasp in position and insert rivets. (Insert all rivets at once.) Turn to back side. Slip washer over each rivet and force it down tight against belt. Lay on metal surface and tap each rivet lightly with hammer until end flattens and holds washer securely (sketch b). Close hasp and fasten with small chain, plastic lacing or padlock (sketch c).

Time required to make: 20 to 30 minutes

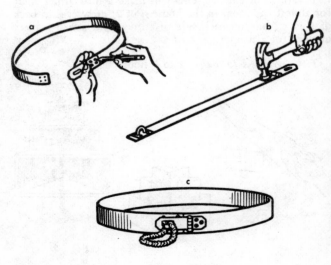

POSTAGE STAMP MOSAIC PICTURES

Materials: Used postage stamps; glue; scissors; pencil; lightweight cardboard (white or pastel shades)

Procedure: Remove stamps from envelopes by soaking in water. Sketch a design on cardboard such as suggested in the illustration. Each design might be made postal-card size or larger for framing. Arrange stamps on design according to color. Trim to fit, if necessary. Glue.

Time required to make: 1½ hours per picture

PARTNERSHIP TREASURE BANK

Materials: 1 coffee or peanut can or 1 pint plastic ice cream container, piece cardboard 1" longer than diameter of container and as deep, pointed can opener (or razor blade for plastic), 1 set foil gummed letters, spray enamel, glue

Procedure: In lid of container make two parallel slits for coins with can opener or razor. Fold cardboard ½" on each side and glue to inside of container to divide it. Put lid on can and spray with enamel. After paint is dry, paste slogan "Lay Up Treasure" made with foil letters around outside of can. Over 1 slot paste "For Me" and over the other slot paste "For God" with foil letters. Good to use to promote tithing or a 50/50 partnership with God.

Time required to make: 20 minutes and drying time

TREASURE CHEST OF BIBLE PROMISES

Materials: A cardboard or metal box approximately 3½" x 2½" x 2½" (if possible, with a hinged lid); metallic paper and glue, or either plaster of Paris or papier-mache; jewels and gold paint; paintbrush; 3 sheets of 8½" x 11" lightweight cardboard (colored if you wish); scissors; ruler

Procedure: Choose 31 Bible promise verses (1 for each day of the month) and mimeograph on lightweight cardboard. Mimeograph so that each verse can be cut out on a 2" x 3" card. Cut Bible promise cards as uniformly as possible (sketch a).

Decorate the treasure chest box attractively by covering with metallic paper, with plaster of Paris or papier-mache (see page 3 for recipe). If you use plaster of Paris, mix one cup with enough water to make a molding consistency. Insert jewels while plaster or papier-mache is pliable. When dry, decorate with gold paint (sketch b).

Insert Bible promise cards (sideways) in finished chest (sketch c).

Time required to make: 1½ to 3 hours

LEATHER OR FELT BELT

Materials: Scraps of leather or felt from craft stores, leather shops or department stores; scissors; needle and thread; snaps or old belt buckles

Procedure: Cut material according to pattern. Number of sections needed will depend upon length of belt. Fold one section in center so that folds fit together. Slip end of next piece through hole and fold over. Continue until belt is desired length. A combination of colors in felt may be used by the girls. Brown and white or black and white leather may be used by boys. For fastening, sew snaps on the felt belt. Slip an old belt buckle on the first section of the leather belt.

Time required to make: 30 to 40 minutes

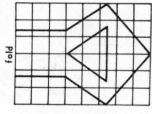

each square = ¼"

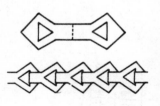

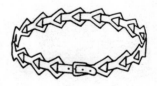

'SICLE SNACK DISH

Materials: 1 heavy cork circle 4" in diameter (heavy cardboard, thin balsa or plywood can also be used), 20 popsicle sticks, Wilhold glue, scissors, shellac, brush

Procedure: Cut circle in half and stand both halves with the flat edge touching table (sketch a). Glue sticks to cork with Wilhold by putting a little glue on the edge of the cork and then placing the stick in place so a little overhangs at each end (sketch a). Glue six sticks in place on each side. Then glue 2 sticks on each side with the narrow edges touching the cork (sketch b). Finish the dish by gluing 4 more sticks across like the first 6 sticks. Do not move dish until dry. Shellac and allow to dry thoroughly before using. Larger dishes can be made by using larger cork circles and more sticks.

Time required to make: 40 minutes and drying time

a

b

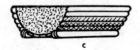

c

SAFETY PIN BRACELET

Materials: 90 small safety pins, stick sealing wax, 7" length round elastic, alcohol lamp or candle, match, clay

Procedure: Exercise care in using an open flame for this project. Groups should be small and there should be a helper. Teacher may hold stick of sealing wax over flame long enough to keep stick soft (not stringy). Pupils close safety pins and dip heads of pins, one at a time, in soft wax, being careful to keep away from flame. Twirl pin to make wax smooth and hold in air a moment to "set." Place closed pin in a lump of clay to dry. Do not touch pins while drying. When thoroughly hardened, string on heavy elastic thread through circle in small end of pin. Tie ends.

Time required to make: 1½ to 2 hours

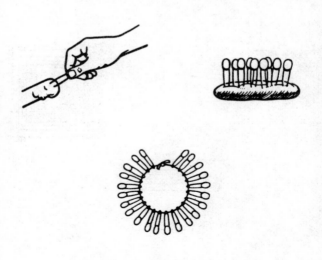

POPSICLE STICK FRAME

Materials: 12 popsicle sticks, 4" square of cardboard, glue, picture of your choice (4" square) which you wish to frame, shellac and brush, gummed hanger or piece of adhesive tape and 4" length of yarn

Procedure: Carefully glue the picture to the cardboard and allow to dry. Measure ¾" from edges and arrange four of the sticks for a frame around the picture. The ends of the sticks should extend about ¼" (see sketch a). Glue in place. Add two sticks to the frame (top and bottom), placing them about half the width of the sticks underneath, and glue securely. Add the sticks to the opposite sides and glue. Continue adding sticks around the picture until all sticks are used and frame is completed (sketch b). Shellac frame carefully. When dry, tape piece of yarn on the back for a hanger (see sketch c). Or, use a gummed hanger.

Time required to make: About 45 minutes

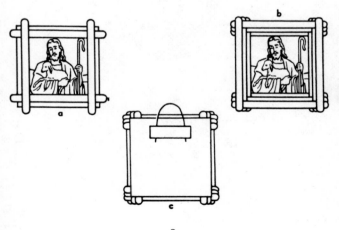

SUJI FIGURES

Suji is a new and fascinating craft featuring colorful, flexible wire as the medium for making figures and ornaments. Kits containing materials and instructions may be obtained from hobby shops. Also you may use scraps of the small colored wire used by telephone companies or board wire used for some types of Data Processing equipment.

Use white glue to hold the ends of the wire in place. Use your imagination and discover how many items can be fashioned from the wire.

10

POPSICLE STICK PLAQUE

Materials: 12 popsicle sticks, glue, piece of cardboard
4½"x4¼", 6" length of yarn for a hanger, Scotch tape,
shellac and brush, macaroni letters or wood-burning pen

Procedure: Lay the twelve sticks side by side and fasten
with two rows of Scotch tape. Cover one side of cardboard
with glue and place ends of yarn on glued surface as
shown in sketch b. Put the taped sticks, taped side down,
on glued cardboard and place under weights to dry.
Choose an appropriate motto and either wood-burn it on
sticks or spell out with macaroni letters. When completed,
shellac and allow to dry.

Time required to make: 30 to 45 minutes

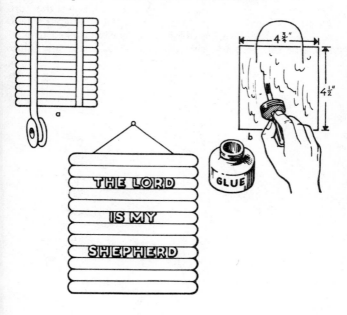

GOURD CRAFT

Materials: All varieties and shapes of gourds, sharp knife, shellac and brush, scraps of felt, cardboard, enamel paint and brush, glue, sandpaper

Procedure: Decide what object you wish to make—a birdhouse, cooky jar, fruit dish or penguin—or a design of your own. Outer skin of gourd must be removed before painting. To do this, soak gourd in water several hours, then rub with sandpaper or a rough pot cleaner. Remove all rough spots. Cut the gourd according to design and clean it out. For a birdhouse cut a hole in the larger portion, near the bottom of the gourd. For a cooky jar and penguin cut off the top. For a fruit dish cut away a portion after you find which way the gourd will best balance as a dish.

After cutting and cleaning the gourd, paint on designs with enamel. If you make a penguin, glue on the top (head) before painting. When dry, give the gourd two coats of shellac. The fruit dish should be shellacked inside, too. For the penguin, cut feet from felt scraps and glue

to body (see pattern, sketch c). It may be necessary to glue the penguin to a cardboard circle to help him stand. Wire the birdhouse to a tree.

Time required to make: 1½ to 2 hours

BEANIE

Materials: Colored felt or wool, scissors, tapestry needle, yarn or mercerized thread, beads and sequins

Procedure: From a strip of felt 6½"x25", follow the pattern and cut six sections (sketch a). Beanie patterns vary according to head sizes. Measure around head and divide by six (six sections). Also measure to crown of head for length needed. Make a paper pattern that fits before cutting felt. Save felt scraps for decorations. From these scraps cut flowers, little musical instruments, stars, Indian designs, etc., and tack on with needle and thread. Or, use beads and sequins as trim. Lace the sections together with yarn or heavy duty mercerized thread and a tapestry needle. Seventeen beanies can be made from one yard of 64" felt. You may combine various colors for each beanie.

Time required to make: 4 to 5 hours

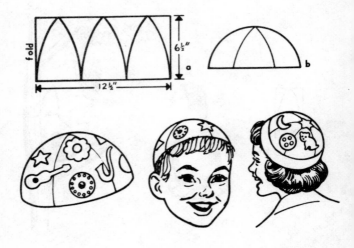

FLYING SAUCER GAME

Materials: A piece of cardboard or plywood 42"x32", masking tape or sandpaper and varnish, 4 small 4" diameter foil pie plates, colored enamel, brush

Procedure: Cut out a triangle whose base is 42" and height 32" for the game board. This is ½ the area of a shuffleboard scoreboard (see sketch). Mark off 5 sections as shown in sketch. Draw in the numbers and paint them a bright color. If you use wood, varnish the board after carefully sanding edges. If you use cardboard, bind the edges with masking tape. Enamel 4 small foil plates different colors. These are the flying saucers.

Object of the game is to obtain highest score. Players must stand 10 ft. from the scoring board and let their saucers fly.

Time required to make: About 2 hours, plus drying time

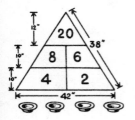

15

MACARONI BRACELET AND PIN

Materials: Small pieces of macaroni, piece of elastic to fit wrist, scrap of felt, safety pins, food coloring, needle and thread

Procedure: Dip macaroni briefly in food coloring. Allow to dry overnight.

For *bracelet* string the macaroni on elastic band. A big safety pin at end of elastic will keep macaroni from slipping off. Sew ends of elastic together.

For *pin* sew macaroni on felt in any design planned, then sew pin to back of felt.

Time required to make: 2 to 2½ hours

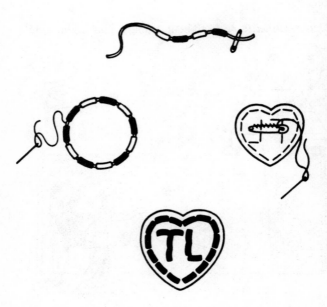

16

PAINTED TILE HOT PADS, PAPERWEIGHTS

Materials: White glazed tile at least 4½″ square; enamel paint; brush; tracing paper; soft lead pencil; masking tape

Procedure: Select or plan a design for your tile and copy on tracing paper (sketch a). Blacken back of design with soft lead pencil. Place blackened side of design on tile, holding it in place with masking tape. Trace over design (sketch b). Paint design with enamel (sketch c). After paint has dried 24 hours, bake tile in oven. Place tile in a cold oven. Gradually increase heat to 300°. Bake 15 minutes at 300°. Turn off heat and allow tile to cool in oven (sketch d).

Time required to make: 1 hour, 10 minutes

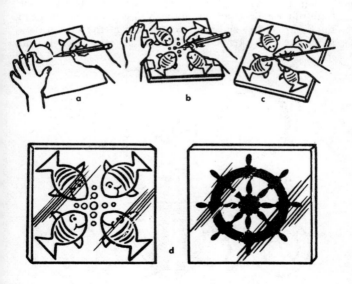

FOREVER CALENDAR

Materials: Piece of colored cardboard 4½"x6", 4 colored cardboard circles 2⅜" in diameter, four ⅜" paper fasteners, pencil, paint, paintbrush, paper punch or ice pick, 10" piece of yarn or ribbon, scissors

Procedure: On the back of the 4½"x6" piece of cardboard mark the center of all four sides. Draw lines connecting the centers of the opposite sides. Cut ½" square windows 1½" in from all four sides (sketch a). Lines connecting sides should go through center of windows. Be sure to measure accurately! Then make a small hole with paper punch or ice pick 1" from each side of the cardboard on the lines connecting sides (sketch a). Turn cardboard over and label the openings as shown in sketch g. Decorate as desired.

Punch a hole in the center of each cardboard circle. Carefully divide one circle into seven equal parts (marking lightly in pencil) and print on the days of the week around the edge (see sketch b). Divide the second circle into

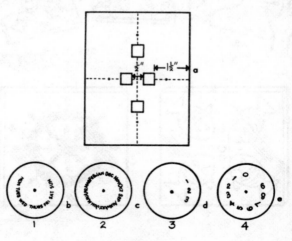

18

twelve equal parts and print on it the months of the year. On the third circle print the numbers 1, 2, 3, as shown in sketch d. Divide the last circle into ten parts and print the numbers 0 through 9 around the edge. With a paper fastener, attach each circle in place on the back of the large cardboard as shown in sketch f, so that the number or word will show through the proper window. Punch two holes in top of calendar. Put one end of yarn or ribbon in each hole and knot on back side (sketch g).

Time required to make: 1 to 1½ hours

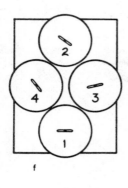

f

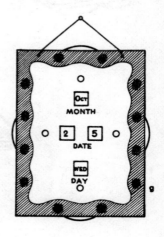

g

SNACK TRAYS

Materials: TV dinner trays (about 6″ x 12″); enamel suitable for painting metal; paintbrush

Procedure: Paint the clean trays any color desired. When dry initials or freehand designs can be painted on the trays. A set of several dozen would be useful for youth groups, church organizations or barbecue parties.

Time required to make: 30 to 60 minutes plus drying time

STRONGBOX

Materials: 1 wooden box and substantial lid to fit it, 2 metal hinges, 1 lock, hammer, screws, nails, varnish, brush, sandpaper, 2 tin can ends

Procedure: Attach lid to box with metal hinges and screws. Sand until smooth, and varnish. Put lock on front. Emboss the two tin can ends by laying them on a block of soft wood and pounding raised initial or design on back with head of nail and hammer. Decorate with a coat of arms design. Nail one embossed circle to center top of strongbox and the other on one end of box. The strongbox in medieval times was used to keep valuables and jewels safe from thieves. Stain or paint it to make it as attractive as possible.

Time required to make: 1 to 2 hours

FISH PURSE

Materials: 2 pieces of light tan burlap 12" x 9½" (or 1 piece 12" x 9½" burlap folded); same amount of red quilted plastic for lining; 1 piece of red burlap 6" x 5" (tail); 2 pieces red burlap 4" x 4" (fins); 1 piece fine fish net 7½" x 12"; 1 cork ball 1" in diameter; sewing materials; crayons or textile paints; scissors; cardboard; pencil; iron; ruler; paper towels; pins; knife

Note: If burlap is not available, wash a gunny sack and bleach it. (This will make several purses.) Dye or paint fins and tail before sewing to fish. If fish net yardage is not available, use mesh vegetable bags.

Procedure: Make cardboard pattern by following sketch a. Cut out and trace pattern on burlap. Draw a design on fish lightly with pencil. Crayon the design or paint with textile paints. If you crayon design, put burlap pieces between paper towels and press with a warm iron to set color. If you use paints allow time for drying, then press. Cut out fish.

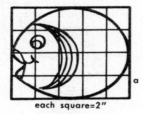

each square=2"

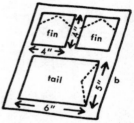

Cut the red burlap tail as shown in sketch b. Pleat tail piece to a 4" width and pin between the 2 burlap sides (right sides facing each other) of the purse, opposite the head. Be sure the tail piece is between purse pieces with only the edge caught in the seam. Sew burlap pieces together ½" from edge. Leave a 6" or 7" opening at top. If sewing is done by hand, sew seams several times with heavy thread (sketch c).

Make pattern ½″ smaller and use to cut out plastic lining. Pin pieces together right sides facing each other (or wrong sides out). Stitch or carefully sew lining pieces together except for a 7″ opening at top of fish. Turn only the burlap piece right side out and press seams with warm iron. Insert plastic lining inside burlap. This puts all seams inside (sketch d).

Make a hole (almost ½″ diameter) through center of the cork ball. Put the piece of net through it lengthwise (sketch e). Place the net ends in each side of the opening of the purse top. Pin net between the burlap and the plastic. Sew or stitch securely (sketch f). The net becomes the purse handle.

Cut one side of the 4″ square red burlap fin pieces to a point as shown in sketch b. Pleat these squares to a 2½″ width and tack on purse in position shown in sketch g.

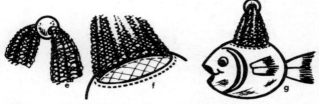

Fringe tail and fin pieces as shown in sketch g. Press purse and it is ready to carry.

Time required to make: 2½ to 4 hours

BONE BELT

Materials: Sliced bones, file, sandpaper, belt, rawhide lacing or thin wire, scissors or wire cutters

Procedure: Have butcher slice bones 3/16″ to ¼″ thick. Boil bones about 15 minutes, scrape off gristle, file rough edges and sand until smooth and white. Tie bone slices to belt with rawhide lacing or thin wire as shown in the sketch or in any original manner.

Time required to make: 45 to 60 minutes

PARROT PLANT HOLDER

Materials: One 14" x 10" piece of ½" wood, coping saw, four brads, five screw eyes, six 6" wire lengths, enamel, brush, wood glue, 6" heavy wire, sheet of paper 14" x 10", ruler, pencil

Procedure: Enlarge pattern and trace on wood (sketch a). Cut out pieces with coping saw. Secure body and head of bird to center of background piece with glue and brads. Fasten wings at either side of body with glue and brads. Paint parrot appropriate colors. Attach screw eye to end of parrot's beak and use heavy wire to make loop through screw eye. Insert three screw eyes at equal distances around outside of shelf disc. Attach two wire lengths to each screw eye as shown in sketch b and fasten in the wire loop suspended from bird's beak. Insert last screw eye at top of background piece for hanging. Any vine or plant will look attractive on the parrot's hanging shelf.

Time required to make: 1½ hours

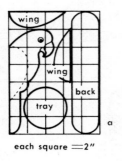

each square = 2"

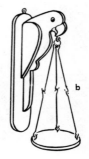

ROLA-PICTURE PURSE

Materials: Large, round oats box; double-pointed knitting needle, size 2; glue; shellac; scissors; heavy material (Indian head), about 8" x 20"; needle; thread; cardboard; narrow grosgrain ribbon or cording 36" long; 1" grosgrain ribbon 19" long, same color as cloth; safety pin; household cement; colored pictures; three rubber bands; darning needle; knife; brush, ruler, pencil

Procedure: Use cardboard pattern and cut about ninety-five triangles, 4" wide and 5" high, from colored shiny magazine pictures. To make into tubes, apply glue in a narrow strip from point of triangle to base (sketch a), and roll triangle on knitting needle beginning with wide end of triangle (sketch b). Slide rolled paper off needle and allow glue to dry.

Cut the oats box to 4" height and glue on tubes vertically, a few at a time. As glue is drying hold tubes in place with rubber bands around box (sketch c). Apply about five coats of shellac to make purse shiny.

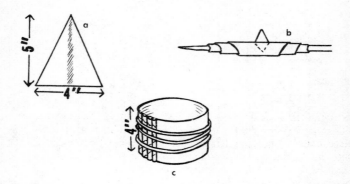

To make drawstring top, cut 8" x 20" piece of cloth in half (8" x 10"). Sew 8" edges together to within 2" of

top of material. Hem last 2″ of seams separately (sketch d). Make a 1″ hem at top of each section. Stitch through middle of this hem to make a ½″ heading for drawstring. Cut 36″ grosgrain ribbon in half. Thread each completely through hem, beginning at opposite sides. Pin a safety pin to end of the ribbon to help push ribbon through. Tie ends together.

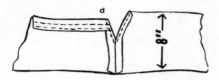

Punch holes with a darning needle ½″ from top of box, one between each two tubes. Fold under the raw edge of cloth top and sew to box by using an over and over stitch through the punched holes (sketch e).

To make binding for bottom of purse, sew two ends of 1″ grosgrain ribbon together with ⅜″ seam. Use a running stitch along one side of ribbon, fit around bottom edge of purse and gather till it fits tightly with gathered side on bottom. Use household cement to glue circle of cardboard to bottom of purse. While cement is drying, place heavy weight inside purse.

Time required to make: 3 to 4 hours

INDIAN NECKLACE

Materials: One 18″ string, 12 small paper or wooden spoons, paint, shellac, brush, paper punch, awl, 11 pieces macaroni or wooden beads

Procedure: Punch or bore hole in each handle. If handles seem too small, bore holes in bowls of spoons. Paint Indian designs on spoons, then shellac. String with a small piece of macaroni or a bead between each spoon. Fasten necklace by tying.

Time required to make: 30 to 45 minutes

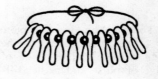

UTILITY SCOOP

Materials: 1 No. 2½-size tin can (or large juice can), 3" end of broom handle, 1" screw, screw driver, Scotch tape, file, tin snips, nail

Procedure: Remove and save label of can. Remove top of can and wash. Punch hole in center of bottom. Fold label in half, blank side out, and draw on design. Cut out and replace label on can, attaching with Scotch tape. Scratch outline on can with nail. Remove pattern. With tin snips cut along line. Smooth edges with file. Start hole in cut end of broomstick with nail. Insert screw from inside can into broomstick handle. Polish scoop to a luster. Decorate with decals if desired. Use for sugar, flour, grain, sand, etc.

Time required to make: 1½ to 2 hours

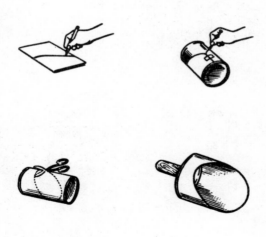

BOOKENDS

Materials: Two 4" x 4" x 1" pieces sanded wood and nails and hammer or plaster of Paris and 1 small cardboard box with lid (gift card box about 4" x 4" is good), 2 figures (Kachinas, totems or South Sea idols made by pupil, see sketches), poster paints or varnish, brushes (For figures: 2 pieces soft wood like balsa or pine 2" x 2" x 6" and carving knives and sandpaper, or pottery clay enough for 2 figures 6" high, or 8 spools, glue, colored construction paper for added features)

Procedure: Make figures for bookends. Make pattern and carve these from wood. Sand and varnish them or paint Kachinas with poster paint. For an unusual finish on South Sea idols, coat them lightly with plaster and let them dry before inserting into plaster base. When base is dry, remove from mold and spray lightly with gold paint. If you do not wish to carve mold two 6" figures from pottery clay. Let them dry until hard. When dry set in plaster base. When plaster is hard, remove bookend from mold, paint with poster paint and varnish lightly with clear

varnish. To make spool totems, glue 4 spools together one on top of the other and let dry. Paint with poster paints. Add colored construction paper features (beaks, wings, etc.). Nail to sanded blocks or set in plaster.

Make plaster base by greasing the inside of cardboard box and lid with Vaseline and then pour in thick creamy mixture of plaster. Just before it sets hard place figure near one edge of each mold. Allow to dry thoroughly then remove cardboard box and rub off any bits of cardboard that remain. If desired, cut and glue felt to cover bottom of plaster bookends. Use for holding missionary books.

Time required to make: 1 to 3 hours depending on type of figure made.

PENDANT AND BUCKLE SET

Materials: Enough patching plaster to fill ½" of 2 sm
sauce dishes, 2 small sauce dishes, Vaseline, 5 paper cli
mixing bowl, water, emery board, paint, brush, lacquer
colorless nail polish, 18" narrow ribbon, enough w
elastic or cloth for around waist, needle, thread, 4 ho
(from hook and eyes)

Procedure: Rub thin film of Vaseline on sauce dish
Mix patching plaster with water to thick consistency a
pour in dishes to ½" depth. When plaster begins to hard
place four paper clips (2 on each side about 1¾" ap
see sketch) in plaster in one dish to make buckle lo
(distance depends upon size of dish.) Place one paper c
in plaster in other dish. When plaster is hard, carefu
remove discs. Wipe off any excess Vaseline and smooth ed
with emery board. Paint matching designs. Tie length
ribbon to pendant. Belt may be made from wide elastic
cloth with hooks sewn in ends at distances to correspo
with loops in buckle.

Time required to make: 30 to 60 minutes

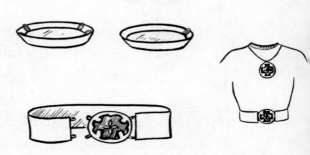

BOW AND ARROW SET

Materials: Hickory or willow dowel 30″ long, ⅜″ diameter; 12″ dowel stick, ¼″ diameter; small suction cup, ⅞″ diameter; sandpaper; varnish; 30″ waxed string or fishing line; 18″ square wrapping paper; crayons; knife

Procedure: Bow: Cut a ½″ notch in each end of long dowel. Work dowel *carefully* into bow by bending, releasing, bending, releasing, until gradual curve is maintained. Fasten waxed string or fishing line in notch at one end of bow. (See sketch.) Bend bow and attach other end of string in same manner, drawing it taut to hold bow in curve. Sand and varnish.

Arrow: Attach small suction cup to dowel stick. Notch opposite end. Extra arrows may be made if desired.

Target: On square of wrapping paper, make a target of three concentric circles: center one red (100 points), middle one blue (50 points), outer one white (25 points). Hang on a wall. Archers stand 15 to 20 feet from target, depending on their skill and strength of the bow. Each player shoots three arrows. Player with highest accumulative score wins.

Time required to make: 1 hour

CLUTCH BAG

Materials: Very stiff cardboard 10" square, 70 yards rug yarn, one large button, 10" x 20" material for lining purse, ice-cream stick, razor blade, scissors, largest size darning needle or bodkin, pencil, ruler

Procedure: Cardboard should be stiff enough so as not to bend when yarn is wound tightly around it. If cardboard bends, paste two or more thicknesses together. Measure and mark every ¼" along top and bottom of cardboard. Cut notches about ¼" deep at each mark (sketch a).

Punch holes with darning needle at opposite corners of cardboard loom. Tie end of yarn through one hole. Wind around loom, placing warp thread through each notch (sketch b). Tie loosely through hole in opposite corner.

With razor blade, carefully notch end of ice-cream stick about ½" deep for shuttle (sketch c). Untie one end of warp thread from hole and tie to three-yard length of weaving thread. Insert other end into shuttle notch. Leading with notched end of stick, begin weaving in and out between each warp thread (sketch d). Weave around the

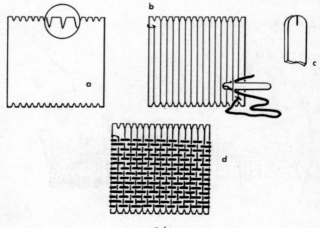

loom on both sides. This will form both front and back of bag at one time. When end of weaving thread is reached, tie on another length of yarn and continue weaving. Allow about 19 yards for warp and 51 yards for weaving. A pattern may be made by using different colors of yarn and different weaving stitches.

Stop weaving within one inch of top of loom. Cut warp threads (sketch e) and tie adjoining warp threads together across width of bag, back and front. When both sides are securely tied, remove weaving from loom. (Untie knot made at beginning of weaving and secure loose end to one of warp threads.) Notice that a wider space appears at both sides of purse. Thread large needle with 20″ of warp yarn and carefully weave in and out an extra warp thread at both sides of bag. Tie thread securely at top. Push all knots through to wrong side and secure with needle and thread so they will not work back to right side when bag is finished.

Fold lining piece in half and sew sides. Fit inside purse, fold edges under and sew in place at top of purse. If you do not wish a fringe at top of bag, fold knotted ends under with lining.

Make loop from yarn and sew at center of one side of bag at top. Fold bag over to desired width and mark place for button. Sew button on, fastening securely through to lining so that buttoning the bag will not damage the weaving (sketch f).

Time required to make: 4 to 5 hours

ZIPPER BAG

Materials: Very stiff cardboard (desired size of bag—suggested size 8" x 10"), 50 yards of rug yarn, 7" zipper, 10" x 14" lining material, ice cream stick, razor blade, scissors, large size darning needle, pencil, ruler

Procedure: Prepare a loom, 8" x 10", as for clutch bag. Follow directions for weaving, ending weaving at least one inch from top of loom. Cut warp threads and tie adjoining threads together. Remove weaving from loom, and weave in an extra strand of warp thread at both sides of bag. Push all knots through to wrong side and sew fast. Fold the lining material in half and sew both sides, allowing ½" seams. Fold top edge down on outside and sew zipper on inside of lining top. With zipper open, sew lining into woven bag. Knotted ends may be left to form fringe, or sewed on the inside with the lining.

Time required to make: 4 to 5 hours

METAL FRUIT DISH

Materials: 1 pie tin (not foil), 1 tuna can, one 1" paper fastener, paint, brush, ice pick, wall-type can opener

Procedure: Remove lid from can with wall-type can opener. Punch hole in center of pie tin and end of can with ice pick. Attach pie tin to can with paper fastener, bending prongs back inside can. Paint and decorate.

Time required to make: 30 minutes

PLASTIC BRACELET

Materials: 3 old toothbrushes of contrasting colors; pliers; hack saw; small vise; drill; glue; nylon elastic thread (heavy); small beads, rhinestones or jewels to fit in bristle holes; ruler

Procedure: Remove all bristles from each toothbrush with pliers. Saw brush into pieces ½" to ¾" long for bracelet links (sketch a). Discard rounded end pieces. Place each link in a vise and drill 4 very small holes, 1 in each corner (sketch b). Lace the bracelet links together with several strands of elastic thread (sketch c). Knot thread ends. Alternate colored plastic using 5 to 7 links (only one jeweled piece). Glue small beads, jewels or rhinestones into bristle holes (sketch d).

Time required to make: 1½ to 2 hours

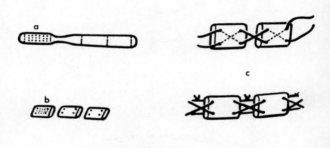

HOUSE NAME SIGN

Materials: Orange crate end, saw, hammer, nails, sandpaper, stain, pencil, ruler, 4 screw eyes, 2 S-hooks, plastic letters, brush

Procedure: Measure wood and mark center. Divide one side in half. Saw boards into three pieces. Sandpaper. Nail narrow pieces at right angle. Stain wood. Tack plastic letters to sign. Attach two screw eyes to sign and two to sign holder. Fasten sign to holder with S-hooks. Nail sign holder to house.

Time required to make: 30 to 60 minutes

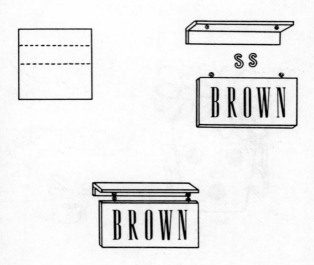

SOUTH SEA ISLAND DOLL PIN

Materials: Thermos cork, two blue, brown or black thumbtacks, one red thumbtack, three gummed reinforcements, staples and stapler, two celluloid rings, a yard of colored yarn, safety pin

Procedure: Trim ⅜" off one side of cork vertically to make back flat. Paste two reinforcements on rounded side of cork for eyes and put two dark thumbtacks inside circles. Place red thumbtack for mouth. Use part of a reinforcement for a nose. Use two staples and two celluloid rings for ears and earrings. For the hair loop the colored yarn back and forth over finger and tie. Affix to top of cork with staple (sketch a). On the back attach a safety pin with another staple (sketch b).

Time required to make: 30 minutes

a

b

BUG LANTERN

Materials: One large fruit juice can, tin snips, block of wood diameter of can, coping saw, puncturing tool, 12" wire, bug repellent candle, enamel, brush, can opener, heavy round stick, pliers, hammer, tacks

Procedure: Remove both ends of can, making cylinder. With tin snips make notches in top of can, approximately 1¾" wide and 2½" deep (sketch a). Make holes in two pointed sections which are opposite each other. Later loop the piece of wire through these holes for hanging. In opposite end of can cut a V-shaped opening large enough to admit candle. With puncturing tool make design in sides of lantern. Fit lantern over a rounded stick to keep it from bending while you are making the design. Prepare plug for bottom by tracing lid on wood block and cutting around outline. Scoop out hole in center the right size to fit candle. Insert plug in bottom of lantern so scooped-out side is on inside. Tack plug in place. With pliers, bend sections at top in toward center (sketch b). Insert wire through holes and fasten into loop. Paint design on sides of lantern. Add candle. Use lantern on porch, lawn, or when camping to keep the bugs away.

Time required to make: 60 minutes

PONCHO BEACH JACKET

Materials: Large bath towel (any color desired), bias tape in contrasting color, needle and thread, scissors, scraps of gingham

Procedure: Fold towel lengthwise and cut along fold 9" beyond center. Bind cut edges with bias tape. Make pockets by folding up cut ends of towel and sewing along sides. Make divisions in pockets with running stitch, sewing securely at top and bottom. Cut four 10" lengths of tape and sew sides to make ties. Tack two ties 10" from end of slit and two more 6" further down. Jackets may be trimmed with gingham applique designs.

Time required to make: 1 hour

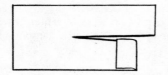

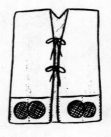

INDIAN SKIRT

Materials: Choose a plain colored material in length and fullness desired, two colors of contrasting bias tape and scraps of two plain materials to match, thread, skirt zipper, snaps, broomstick (length of skirt), string, skirt pattern, scissors, needle, thread, straight pins, sewing machine

Procedure: Follow pattern which calls for a 3" or 4" band and gathered skirt and make skirt. Sew several rows of colored tape alternately above hem. Applique on skirt several squares (or other designs) of cloth which matches braid. When skirt is completed, dip in warm water and squeeze, then carefully wrap around broom handle and tie. When dry, the skirt will be "Indian pleated."

Variation in design can be obtained by decorating unbleached muslin skirt with crayons and pressing with hot iron.

Time required to make: 4 or 5 hours

STENCILED SCARF, T-SHIRT OR BLOUSE

Materials: Unbleached muslin 20" x 20", scarf from home, T-shirt or blouse, stenciling paint (We suggest you try Tri Chem Pen paints. They come in tubes equipped with ball point ends and are available at hobby and art stores. Designs are drawn on cloth by using tube as you would a pen or crayon), or textile paint, stencil brush, stencil designs, iron, thumbtacks, newspapers, pencil

Procedure: Tack fabric down taut to hard surface over several layers of newspaper and trace design on it. Paint over design with paints of desired colors. Set colors with hot iron. A fringe may be made around scarf if muslin is used. Towels, wash cloths, dish towels, etc., may also be decorated.

Time required to make: 30 to 60 minutes

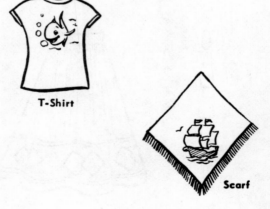

T-Shirt

Scarf

44

CAN CAMP STOVE

Materials: Two large tin cans, one slightly larger than the other; two can openers, one juice, one cutter type; tin snips; heat tablet

Procedure: Cut top from larger can, leaving smooth edges. Make vent holes with juice can opener (sketch a). Cut other can to 3" height. With juice can opener, cut V-shaped holes in bottom. With tin snips, cut out legs for platform (sketch b). Place heat tablet in bottom of large can with platform over tablet (sketch c). Legs should not cover vent holes. Light heat tablet through one vent hole. Camp stove is ready to heat opened cans of food.

Time required to make: 30 minutes

COOK-OUT STOVE

Materials: 1 large pie tin (not foil), 1 gallon tin can with one end removed, one 1″ paper fastener, ice pick, tin snips

Procedure: Make several holes in each side of gallon can with punch-type can opener. Punch hole in center of pie tin and in end of gallon can with ice pick. Fasten tin to can with paper fastener. Cut 4″ square opening in one side of can. When building fire, place stove so that opening faces breeze.

Time required to make: 30 minutes

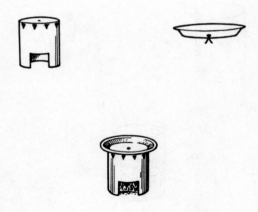

COOK-OUT BRAZIER

Materials: 1 large square oil can, tin snips, oven rack or grill

Procedure: Obtain a large oil can. Cut down center of one side and across ends. Bend cut sections to sides of can. For fire, use charcoal and a little wood. Place oven rack or metal grill over top.

Time required to make: 20 to 30 minutes

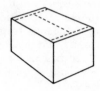

BEACH BAG

Materials: Cotton fabric 15" x 36" (duck, denim or sail-cloth), 12" x 36" plastic for lining, felt scraps or other contrasting fabric, thread, 10" zipper or four buttons, needle or sewing machine

Procedure: From fabric cut strip 3" x 36" for strap. Fold inside out, lengthwise. Sew edges together and turn right side out.

Plan design to fit an 11" x 10" space for outside of bag. Cut design from scraps and sew on right side of material. (See sketches for suggested design.)

Placing right sides of fabric and plastic together, sew up sides to form tube. Turn right side out. Fold tube cross-wise and push bottom up to form two pockets inside bag (see sketch a). Tack in place. Turn raw edges at ends of tube inside to 2" or 3" depth. Sew lining and fabric together. Sew zipper across top of bag (stitching through both fabric and lining) or add buttons and buttonholes.

Secure both sides of bag with blanket stitch. Finish neatly at top so zipper ends are concealed. Sew ends of shoulder strap to top corners of bag (sketches b and c).

Time required to make: 2 hours

NYLON WATER LILY

Materials: Fine wire (10 feet for each flower); three pieces 10" long, six pieces 9" long, three pieces 7" long and three pieces 2½" long (extra piece is for fastening leaves and petals together); green plastic tape; heavy white thread; two nylon stockings; dye remover and green dye; few yellow stamens, scissors

Procedure: Cut foot and top from stockings and cut down seam. Make one stocking white by placing in dye remover. Dye the other one a medium green. Bend the three pieces of 10" wire to form leaves, and twist (sketch a). Do the same with the 9", 7" and 2½" lengths. Cut three pieces of green nylon, stretch tightly over the wire leaves and tie firmly with thread. Cover the remaining wire petals with white nylon and tie. The tighter the nylon is stretched, the prettier the flower will be (sketch b). Arrange the three smallest white petals around a few stamens and tie with thread, then with wire. Arrange the three next size white petals and tie. Add the six largest petals last. Wire all together firmly and cover about one-half inch down with green plastic tape. Add the three green leaves. Wire these securely to the petals and cover with plastic tape (sketch c). This lovely lily can be placed in a flower bowl or worn as a corsage. White stocking may be dyed any pastel shade for different types of flowers.

Time required to make: 60 minutes

TALCUM FLOWER

Materials: Can of talcum powder, red and green crepe paper, Scotch tape, red ribbon, scissors

Procedure: Cut crepe paper 1" wider than height of can and long enough to wrap around can 3 times. Wrap red paper around can, with extra width of paper at top of can, and secure with tape. Wrap green paper around red paper and tape. Tie red ribbon around can. Cut green paper in 3 points and fold back. Cut red paper to top of can in ½" strips. This makes a lovely talcum flower from which to shake powder.

Time required to make: 30 minutes

MAGAZINE WALL FILE

Materials: 3 wire clothes hangers, pliers, enamel, brush, tin snips

Procedure: Snip off the hooks of two hangers and bend hook of third to form circle. Use pliers to straighten hangers, then bend as shown in sketch a. Enamel. Hang one over other (sketch b) and they are ready to use (sketch c).

Time required to make: 30 to 45 minutes

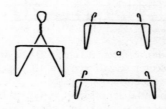

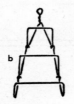

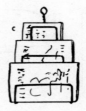

PAJAMA JESTER

Materials: Piece of material 15"x30", clean white sock, clean nylon hose (old), colored yarn or small bell, 12" length of colored ribbon 2" wide, needle and thread, pinking shears, pins, string, paint or embroidery floss

Procedure: Enlarge pattern from sketch. Lay pattern on material and pin in place. Cut out. Allowance has been made for seams.

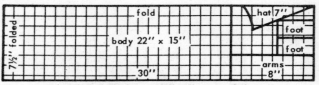

each square=1"   Arms: 2½"x8"; feet: 3½"x 1¾".

BODY: Fold sides to meet in center. Baste or press edges back. Stitch up center seam leaving a 10" opening. Stitch on wrong side across bottom and gather.

ARMS: Fold material lengthwise, wrong side out. Stitch across one end and up sides. Turn right side out. To attach arms, cut 1¼" slits in body material on each side, 5½" from center slit and 4½" from top. Insert open end of arm. On wrong side stitch across opening, catching arm.

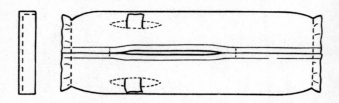

FEET: Cut feet from material with pinking shears. Put two feet together, right sides out, and stitch around sole, leaving end of heel open. Stuff foot with old nylon hose or other material. Sew up heel. Sew foot at X to gathered end of body.

HEAD: Cut 5″ cuff from white sock and stuff toe of sock with nylon hose to form the head. Tie with string at neck. Gather around top of body material. Insert end of sock and pull gathers. Sew head firmly in place.

HAT: Fold material wrong side out so straight sides are together. Sew sides together. Turn right side out. Arrange on head and tack in place, turning edge under. Bell or tassel of yarn may be added to point of hat.

FINISHING: Make generous ruffle from ribbon or any stiff material and tack around neck. Embroider or paint face on jester. Place pajamas in bag and tie arms.

Time required to make: 2 to 3 hours

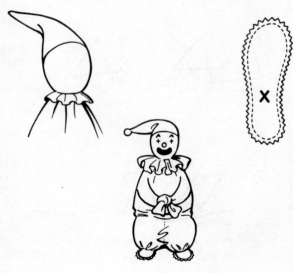

WIRE BOOK HOLDER

Materials: 2 wire clothes hangers, solder, soldering iron, string, newspaper, enamel, brush, steel wool, pliers, tin snips

Procedure: Snip off the hooks of two metal hangers below twist. Straighten wires, then bend them as shown in sketch a. Solder loose ends together. Place together as shown in sketch b. Scrape off paint at points that touch with steel wool. Tie sections together with string at point A and B. Solder at points C and D. When dry, remove string and solder at points A and B. (Work on a thick layer of newspapers so that enamel and solder do not ruin any surfaces.)

Time required to make: 60 minutes

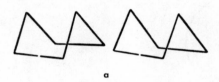

a

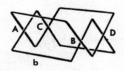

b

SNACK TRAY

Materials: 2 wire coat hangers, wire cutter, 11" diameter wood disc, 14 staple tacks, hammer, varnish or enamel, decals, awl, pliers, brush, newspapers

Procedure: Bore hole in center of disc. Enamel or varnish. Cut hooks from coat hanger 1½" from twisted section. Discard one. Measure 2¾" from each rounded end of hangers and bend over table at right angle to form legs. Place one set of legs across under side of disc and fasten with staple tacks as shown in sketch. Fasten the second set of legs in the same way. Insert hook from top of disc, bend ends back on under side and staple. Apply decals.

Time required to make: 30 to 60 minutes

MARIONETTE

Materials: Two pieces pine lumber, one ¾" x ¾" x 16", the other ¾" x 1¾" x 5½"; twenty-six screw eyes; three nails; four ruler-width control sticks, one 15" long, one 12" long and two 9" long; sandpaper; saw; linen thread; poster paint; brush; cardboard; brace and bit; hammer, ruler, pencil

Procedure: Cut head and body from lumber ¾" x 1¾" x 5½" (sketch a). Cut arms, legs and feet from lumber

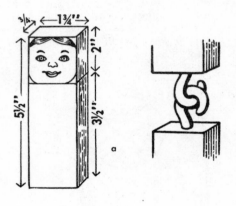

¾" x ¾" x 16" as shown in sketch b. Round off all joints with sandpaper. Put pieces together with screw eyes interlinked. Use two screw eyes for ears. Draw face, and paint. Hands may be made from cardboard. Drill a small hole in the center of control boards A, B and C. Pound three nails through board D allowing them to extend at least ½" through board (sketch c). Place boards A, B and C over these nails to hold them in place while the puppet is being operated. To string puppet attach linen threads to

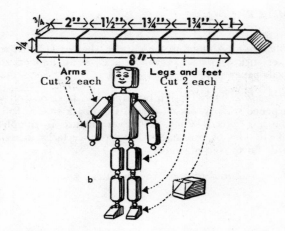

Arms
Cut 2 each

Legs and feet
Cut 2 each

b

knee joints and to both ends of control board A, hands to board B, head to board C, and shoulders toward back of board D (sketch c). Make a suit (or have ladies of the church furnish this) and dress doll.

Time required to make: 1½ to 2 hours

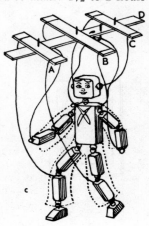

c

FOIL CRAFT

Materials: Aluminum or copper sheet foil, sharpened sucker stick, newspapers, fancy tacks, scrap lumber, stain, pencil, paper

Procedure: Draw design on paper and trace on foil with sharpened stick. Work on design from back side of foil for embossing effect. When plaque or picture is completed, fold all sides of foil and tack with fancy tacks to stained board. Encourage ingenuity.

Time required to make: 60 minutes

BOOK HOLDER

Materials: 3 orange crate ends, saw, small nails, hammer, sandpaper, pencil, enamel, brush

Procedure: Saw one crate in half, diagonally. Saw off ¼ of another end and discard. Sandpaper all pieces. Nail the ¾ crate end to the uncut end at a right angle. Place corner of each end of nailed pieces in center of long side of diagonally cut pieces and mark with pencil. Turn diagonally cut pieces over and nail to sides of shelf. Paint.

Time required to make: 30 to 60 minutes

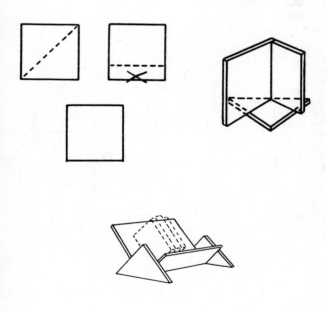

CLOTHES BAG

Materials: 1 piece of paper for a pattern about 10" x 12", 1 pencil, ruler or yardstick, straight pins, piece of printed material about 10" x 24", scissors, scraps of flesh-colored material, 4 buttons, needle, thread, cotton

Procedure: Make paper patterns. Cut pants and suspenders of print material (sketch a). Cut two pieces of flesh-colored material for each foot (sketch b). Sew feet first, right sides together. Turn, stuff. Baste feet to right side of one pants section (sketch c). Place second section on top, right side down. Stitch feet and pants in one seam leaving waist open. Hem waistline and turn right side out. Put suspenders right sides together and stitch long edges. Turn, press and sew onto pants. Add buttons (sketch d).

Time required to make: 1½ to 2 hours

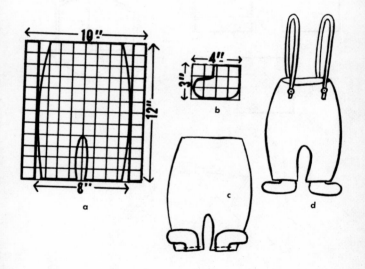

SHELF-N-COAT RACK

Materials: 1 apple crate, sandpaper, saw, nails, paint, brush, hammer, 3 small screw coat hooks

Procedure: Remove one side of crate. Saw ends in half diagonally. Sandpaper and paint. Nail to wall, screw in hooks. Shelf may be used for books or hats; hooks for coats.

Time required to make: 40 to 60 minutes

RELIEF MAP

Materials: Soapsuds paint (see page 113), waxed paper, piece of plywood or heavy cardboard size of map desired, sandpaper or binding tape, knife, flat sucker stick, paint, paintbrush, pencil

Procedure: Bind the edge of cardboard for map base, or sand edges of plywood. Outline map on board with pencil. Apply soapsuds paint in layers to show topography of country, such as Palestine, Bible Lands, Mediterranean Lands, etc. Slightly moisten hands when shaping mountains, etc.

Fresh soapsuds paint can be added to the dry part without danger of cracking. Be sure to allow each layer to dry before applying the next. Use the knife and stick to draw in rivers, shape mountains, etc. When dry, paint lakes, rivers, mountains, etc.

Time required to make: About 2 hours

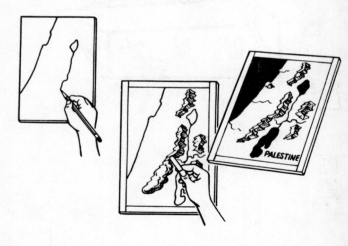

BELT, WRISTBAND, OR COLLAR SET

Materials: For belt or wristband: an old belt, a wristband or piece of leather and buckle, sharpened sucker stick, aluminum foil, scissors, adhesive tape, decorated tacks or ½" paper fasteners, ice pick, pliers

For collar: 12" x 15" colored felt, pinking shears, two 8" lengths ribbon, needle, matching thread, ¼" paper fasteners

Procedure: For belt: make designs on aluminum foil medallion (or have friends initial medallions). Cut out and attach to leather belt with decorated tacks or paper fasteners. (Make holes in belt with ice pick.) If tacks are used, bend point back with pliers on wrong side. Cover tack points or paper fastener prongs with adhesive tape. IDEA: Use only tacks or paper fasteners and make studded design on belt.

Fellows may follow the same idea in making wristbands as used in decorating belts.

For collar: girls may cut out round collars from felt with pinking shears and decorate with ¼" paper fasteners. Tack strips of ribbon on for tie.

Time required to make: 30 to 60 minutes on each project

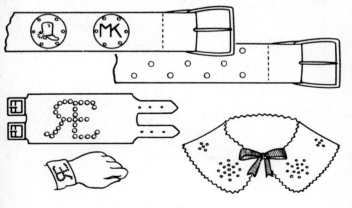

BOOKWORM

Materials: One 12" chenille wire, felt scraps, thread the same color as scraps, needle, sequins, small beads, cotton, paper clip, glue, pencil, paper for pattern

Procedure: Cut felt twice as large as pattern. Overcast body pieces together along saw-toothed edge, sewing beads to spine. Add bright beads for eyes and sequins for decoration. Insert chenille wire so that 1" sticks out at X and rest of it goes through body and out point marked XX. Stuff body with cotton and sew to bottom. Sew paper clip below XX. (See sketch.) Curve wire on top of worm's head; glue sequin to end. Clip bookworm to outside of book and bend wire tail to mark place in book.

Time required to make: 30 to 45 minutes

Body cut 2

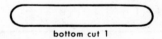

bottom cut 1

BULLETIN BOARD

Materials: Sheet cork 24" x 30"; plywood 24" x 30"; household cement; tacks; friction tape or Mystik Tape; picture wire; screw eyes; rope, braid or ruffling

Procedure: Mount cork on plywood with household cement and tacks. Bind edges with colored friction tape or Mystik tape. Let young people use their creative abilities to gaily decorate bulletin boards. Use ruffles, rope, braid, etc., to finish borders. Insert screw eyes in back of upper corners, two inches from top and attach picture wire. Hang in bedroom or kitchen.

Time required to make: 30 to 60 minutes

POP-OUT PICTURE

Materials: Action picture, poster board, cardboard frame, paint or crayons, brush, glue, cloth, leather, pencil, scissors

Procedure: Select or draw a simple action picture the same size as the picture frame. Trace figures on poster board..Paint and add cloth, leather, etc., where appropriate. Arrange figures in picture so that action forces some out of frame (see sketches). Fill in background with scenery and glue the figures in proper places.

Time required to make: 30 to 60 minutes

SHIP'S LANTERN

Materials: No. 2½ tin can, tin snips, bailing wire, hammer, nail, solder and soldering iron or paper fastener, candle, friction tape, bottle cap

Procedure: Cut can with tin snips or old household scissors (Sketch a). Use wire to fashion handle after holes have been made with hammer and nail. Fasten bottle cap in bottom of can with solder, or make holes in cap and can and attach with paper fastener. Fit candle into cap (sketch b). If desired, the wire handles can be fastened to light cord with friction tape so that globe will hang in lantern for light.

Time required to make: 30 minutes

67

FOIL BELT

Materials: Heavy aluminum foil (or foil pans), pencil or orange stick, two pieces of cord long enough to tie in bow around waist, pliers, scissors, punch

Procedure: Design link pattern and measure around waist to estimate number of links needed (about 6 or 8). Trace pattern on foil, allowing two pieces for each link. Cut out pieces carefully. Hold two foil pieces together and use pliers to bend edges under ⅛". Press folded edges tightly together with pliers, so that no rough edges will remain. The double thickness of foil will make a strong link.

Make designs or initials or spell out name on links. (See sketch.) Make design by pressing on links with pencil or orange stick. Background may be stippled with pencil point to give the design a raised effect.

On opposite sides of links punch two holes about ½" apart for lacing. Lace links with cord, leaving ends long enough to tie around waist. (Foil covered cord to match links may be purchased at dime stores.)

Time required to make: 2 to 2½ hours

TIN CAN PLANTER

Materials: 2 pieces scrap wood 3" x 6½", large fruit juice can, coping saw, enamel, brush, tin snips, hammer, 4 medium nails with large heads, enough·soil to fill planter, plants or artificial floral materials, one 3" x 7" sheet of paper for pattern, pencil, sandpaper, glue or wax

Procedure: Cut juice can in half lengthwise with tin snips (see sketch a). From sketch b make pattern, trace and cut out wooden stands. Sand them. Fasten half of can to stands with large-headed nails. Make holes leakproof with glue or wax. Paint blocks and can with a good enamel. Add any design you may wish. Fill planter with dirt. Place plant or artificial flora in planter.

Time required to make: 60 minutes

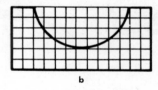

MESH BAG

Materials: One copper pot cleaner (if you purchase the large size, use one-half for bag and one-half for beanie, or make two bags from small size); piece of plain, bright silk material (taffeta, satin, etc.) 1½" less than depth of mesh for bag and ½" longer than circumference; large and small eye needles; thread; 10 small brass rings; 1 yd. narrow ribbon to match material or 1 yd. gold braid for drawstring handles

Procedure: Unstaple pot cleaner and carefully stretch to full size. Cut in half and save one half for making matching beanie or another bag. Unravel 3 strands of the pot cleaner. Gather one end of tube by weaving strand in and out. Draw strand tight and tie it. Roll edge of opposite end and tack with another strand of copper thread.

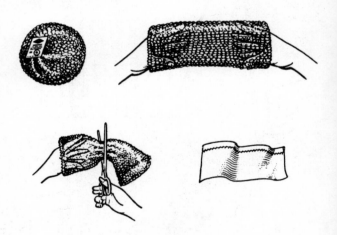

Make ¼" hem along one long side of the silk. Sew the narrow sides together. Gather unhemmed end of material and secure. Insert gathered end of material into copper bag for lining and tack gathered ends of silk and copper

bag together. With another strand of pot cleaner, threaded in a large eye needle, tack top edge of lining about 1½" from top edge of copper mesh bag. Around outside of bag at lining edge, sew small brass rings at equal intervals. If rings are pinned in place first (about 1" apart), they can be spaced more easily. Cut ribbon in half. Slip 1 half through rings and tie ends together. Run other half of ribbon through rings, starting at opposite side of first handle. Tie ends. Draw both handles tight.

Time required to make: 45 minutes to 1 hour

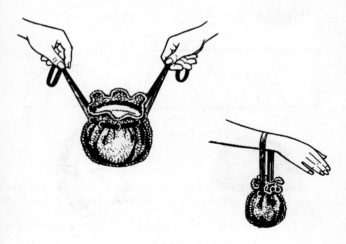

MESH BEANIE

Materials: One-half of copper pot cleaner, large size; colored wool, felt or silk (1" less than depth of mesh and ½" longer than circumference) to match mesh bag lining (17 beanies can be made from 1 yd. of 64" felt); needle and thread

Procedure: STYLE 1: From strip of felt or wool, follow the pattern and cut six sections. Measure around head to determine correct head size. Sew the panels together with small stitches. Unravel 2 strands of copper thread from pot cleaner. Gather end of pot cleaner and secure. (See instructions under "Mesh Bag.") Roll opposite edge and tack with copper thread. Roll should be on outside. Tack mesh beanie over felt. Cover a large button with a piece of the silk and tack on top of beanie.

STYLE 2: Make the silk beanie lining the same way as the mesh bag lining. (See "Mesh Bag.") Tack it inside the mesh covering at the gathered end and then near the edge of the rolled hem. Add covered button.

Time required to make: 45 minutes to 1 hour

HOUSE NUMBER SIGN

Materials: End of 1 orange crate, scrap of wood 2" x 12", sandpaper, coping saw, enamel, brush, house numbers, finishing nails, pencil, ruler

Procedure: Draw design on wood. Cut out with coping saw. Cut stake piece 12" x 2" with pointed end. Sandpaper and paint. Tack numbers on "house" or numbers may be painted. Nail stake to back of sign.

Time required to make: 30 to 60 minutes

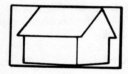

ROOSTER BOOK HOLDER

Materials: 1 wire coat hanger, one 2" styrofoam ball, 1 red pipe cleaner, ½ yellow pipe cleaner, 2 sequins of the same color, 2 straight pins

Procedure: Take the center of the hanger's cross wire and the hook and pull them away from each other to straighten and elongate the hanger (see sketch a). Lay the hanger on a flat surface and bend both wires up at right angles about 4" from the hook and bend up at right angles again about 5" from the first bend. The hanger should be U-shaped and the hook should face away from the center of the U (see sketch b). Push the styrofoam ball onto the hook. Accordion pleat the red pipe cleaner and insert into ball for comb (sketch c). Bend the yellow pipe cleaner and push into ball at the right place for beak. Pin 1 sequin on each side for eyes (sketch d). To use the bookholder, place books upright in the rooster's back.

Time required to make: 30 minutes

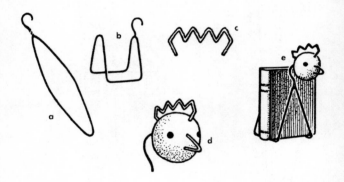

74

CARRYALL PICNIC KIT

Materials: One large and one small bandanna in matching colors, three 27" white shoestrings, needle and thread, 24 small metal or bone rings, a 1 lb. coffee can, enamel, several aluminum foil plates, plastic knife, fork, spoon.

Procedure: To make the carryall bag, sew the 24 rings on the wrong side of the large bandanna in a circle about 5" apart, starting approximately 1" from the sides. From two opposite corners, run shoestrings through rings and tie. Fold small bandanna up 5" and sew 3 pockets at one side, each 1½" wide for silverware. Sew shoestring in center of opposite side.

Place can in carryall bag to hold lunch. If plates are larger than can, place under it, otherwise place over can. Put silverware in pockets, fold top over, roll and tie. Place in can.

Time required to make: 30 to 60 minutes

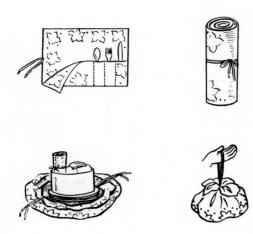

TIER BOOKCASE

Materials: ¾" lumber cut to sizes 8" x 48", 8" x 36", 8" x 24"; two pieces 8" x 9"; four doorstops; four dowel sticks ¾" x 9"; 1½" finishing nails; stain; varnish or enamel; brush, sandpaper; hammer; ruler, pencil

Procedure: Measure 18" from one end of the 48" board. Set a dowel stick about 2½" in from each side and nail from opposite side of board. (Dowel sticks should stand erect.) Nail one 9" piece to opposite end of shelf, making sure the edges are square. Follow same procedure with 36" shelf piece. Fit 36" shelf on top of the dowels and upright board of 48" shelf, so that the solid uprights are at opposite ends. Nail the 36" shelf to the dowels and upright upon which it rests. Nail the 24" board on top to form the top shelf. Screw doorstops in the bottom of the 48" shelf 12" from each end, and 2½" from edges for legs. (If you have wood drilling equipment, bore holes ½" deep for dowel sticks and secure with glue instead of using nails. Dowel sticks should then be 10" long.) Sandpaper shelves. Stain, varnish or enamel as desired.

Time required to make: 2 hours

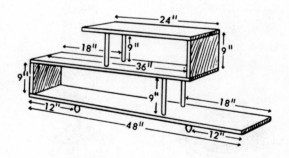

TROUSER TREE

Materials: Piece of wood 14" x 10", four ¾" wooden strips approximately 2" x 14", eight 1½" flat-headed screws, two nails or screws at least 3" long, coping saw, sandpaper, stain, shellac or enamel, brush, pencil, piece of paper 14" x 10", ruler

Procedure: Make enlarged paper pattern and trace on 14" x 10" piece of wood. Cut out with saw (sketch a). Sandpaper until smooth. Screw the four strips to the cut piece forming a stairstep arrangement (sketch b). Stain the trouser tree any desired color, and finish with a coat of shellac. The tree may also be enameled, then decorated with contrasting paint or decals. Tree may be fastened to a closet door or to a wall. Hang trousers carefully over tree arms to keep them in crease.

Time required to make: 1½ hours

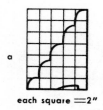

each square = 2"

b

HANDY BOOKRACK

Materials: Wooden box, saw, screws or nails, screw driver, hammer, scrap lumber, wood glue, stain and varnish or enamel, brush, sandpaper

Procedure: Saw box in half diagonally, as shown in sketch. If box is equally usable on all sides, two bookracks can be made from one box. Use triangular pieces of scrap lumber (approximately the same size as the ends of the bookrack) to make standards. Fasten one triangle to each end of bookrack as shown in sketch. Attach with glue, then fasten with screws or nails. Sand the bookrack and finish with stain and varnish or enamel.

Time required to make: 60 minutes

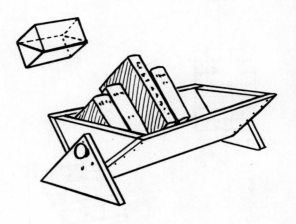

BIRD'S SNACK SHELF

Materials: Two pieces of wood such as barrel ends (or other shapes), one piece of wood 2" x 2" x 13", one large screw eye, one 2" screw, screw driver, 10" hardware cloth, wire or heavy cord, paint, brush

Procedure: Mark center of both wood pieces. Insert screw eye through center of one disc, then into one end of 13" piece of wood for top of snack bar. Screw other disc to opposite end of block with 2" screw. Paint or decorate as desired. Make pocket of hardware cloth around bottom of pole to hold scraps for birds. Tie wire or cord to screw eye and hang shelf from a tree branch.

Time required to make: 60 minutes

bird's snack shelf

KEYBOARD

Materials: Scrap lumber, sandpaper, coping saw, pencil, 8 or 10 screw hooks, varnish or paint, brush, 2 screw eyes, wire

Procedure: Draw a large key on lumber and cut out with coping saw. Sandpaper. Mark places for screw hooks and print labels on board to identify keys. Paint or varnish. Put screw hooks on keyboard. Hang up by wire.

Time required to make: 60 minutes

keyboard

VOLLEY RACKET

Materials: Plywood 11" in diameter, coping saw, strip of leather or denim 1" x 6", sandpaper, stapler (or hammer and tacks), material 6" wide and 20 feet long for net

Procedure: Cut wood in shape of racket. Sand. Tack or staple leather or denim strip across one side to slip hand under (see sketch). Be sure strap is not too tight or too loose. Make court 50 feet long and 15 to 20 feet wide. For net, stretch cloth at height of 6 feet. Use tennis ball and play racket volley like volleyball.

Time required to make: 30 minutes

FOIL JEWEL BOX

Materials: Two aluminum-foil pans of same size (preferably square or oblong), 24" of narrow ribbon, rug yarn or fancy shoelace, scraps of material for lining, glue, punch, enamel (optional)

Procedure: Glue material inside both pans for lining. Punch evenly spaced holes along adjoining edge of each pan, allowing ¼" margin. Lace pans together to form box, making sure that edges fit firmly. (See sketches.) Box may be used for jewelry, buttons, handkerchiefs or gloves.

Variation: Stipple or enamel outside of pans and decorate lid with a design or Scripture verse. When enamel is dry, line pans with material and lace together.

Time required to make: 30 to 60 minutes

KNICKKNACK SHELF

Materials: Two orange crate ends, sandpaper, 42 spools same size, awl, three 24" lengths wire, six bottle caps, 1 nail, hammer, 2 screw eyes, strong cord, saw, enamel or varnish, brush

Procedure: Saw crate squares in half diagonally and sandpaper three pieces. Bore small hole in each corner. Make two holes in bottle caps with nail. Run wire through hole in one corner of a board and one hole in bottle cap, leaving about 1" of wire. Return wire through other hole in bottle cap and through board. Twist securely, then string 7 spools between shelves. Put wire through bottle cap and fasten. Attach screw eyes to top shelf and fasten string for hanging. Varnish or enamel.

Time required to make: 30 to 60 minutes

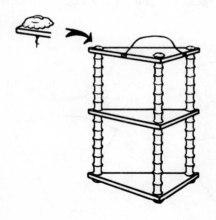

WORDLESS WORLD PIN

Materials: 2 lightweight cardboard circles 2" diameter, one 2" square and one 1" square black felt, one 2" square and one 1" square white felt, two 1" squares gold felt, one 1" square each of these colors: green, blue, red; 1 paper fastener, scissors, pencil, very small safety pin, paper punch, three 5" strands lightweight red yarn, Wilhold glue

Procedure: Cover one 2" cardboard circle with 2" square black felt. Glue together and trim edges. Trace outline of map (sketch a) onto white felt, cut out and glue to black circle. Punch hole in center of black circle and through top ¼" in from edge. Trace fish, the symbol of the early Christians (sketch b), on 1 piece gold felt and cut out. Put the 3 strands of red yarn through top hole and double. Braid 1" length of braid. Tie end in knot and slip safety pin through knot. Glue fish to pin and knot and set aside to dry.

Trace triangle (sketch c) and cut 1 triangle from each of

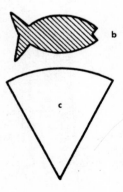

84

the remaining colors. Place triangles clockwise in this order: black (sin), red (Christ's blood), white (clean heart), gold (heaven), green (grow in Christ), blue (witness or separation), and glue in place. Trim edges if needed. Allow to dry and then punch hole in center of circle. Cut smaller triangle from world circle as indicated in sketch d. Put fastener through world circle and then through the colored circle and fasten loosely at the back.

d

Use to tell Wordless Book story. Wear with black triangle showing through upper slit. Teacher may wish to make larger world from paper for class use.

Time required to make: 30 to 45 minutes

STIPPLE PICTURE

Materials: Scrap lumber or orange crate end, stain, coping saw, small nails or tacks, large nail, hammer, enamel, 2 screw eyes, wire, tin can, tin snips, file, brush

Procedure: Cut wood base to desired shape, sandpaper and stain. Remove ends from can and cut along seam. Cut piece of tin desired shape for mounting on wood. Scratch design on tin with nail. Make large nail blunt (place nail point on cement and hit with hammer). Place tin on what will be wrong side of wood base and stipple design with hammer and blunt nail. File edges of tin and paint around design. Tack stipple picture on wood. Attach screw eyes and wire on back for hanging.

Time required to make: 30 to 60 minutes

COPPER WIRE JEWELRY

Materials: About 12" medium copper wire, 1 pretty rock or semi-precious stone such as agate, etc., long-nosed pliers, clear nail polish or lacquer and brush

Procedure: Wrap copper wire around the stone in several directions and twist together at the top to hold stone in place and give a loop for fastening to chain, bracelet or key chain (sketch a). Coat the wire and stone with clear nail polish or lacquer to keep from tarnishing.

Time required to make: 20 to 30 minutes

SLAVE BRACELET

Materials: Two or three pieces of heavy aluminum foil (or foil pans) approximately 7″ x 1½″, stippling tool (large nail or any pointed instrument), pencil, pliers, scissors, enamel, lacquer, paper, brush

Procedure: Draw pattern for bracelet and cut two or three pieces of foil according to the pattern. (Three pieces make a heavier bracelet.) Draw a design on paper and trace on smooth foil for outside of bracelet. Stipple background so design will stand out (sketch a). Hold all pieces of bracelet together with edges even. With pliers fold edges under ⅛″ all around bracelet. Press tightly to make edges smooth. Bend bracelet into an oval shape, leaving ends open (sketch b). If inside edges are not smooth, work around bracelet again with pliers.

If desired, enamel design with bright colors. To protect enamel, add clear lacquer or nail polish when enamel is dry.

Time required to make: 1 to 1½ hours

PERSONALIZED SCARF

Materials: Silk scarf, crayons, iron, newspapers

Procedure: Fold scarf into 2" squares. (If name is more than 8 letters, divide scarf into more squares.) Print name along top of scarf (see sketch). Use a different color for each letter. Finish line by repeating as many letters as space allows. Begin next line with letter that precedes first letter in the line above. Repeat until letters are marked on all rows. This makes a pattern of the same letters in the same color diagonally across the scarf. Place the scarf on a newspaper with the crayon side down. Set color with a warm iron. Do not slide iron or color will blur.

Time required to make: 60 minutes

ORIENTAL SHOES

Materials: Wrapping paper; ends of orange or apple crates; coping saw; sandpaper; 2 blocks 2½"x1½"x½"; 2 blocks 1½"x1½"x½"; 10 nails 1" long; 12 tacks; hammer; 2 pieces of ribbon (or canvas) ½" wide, 15" long; 2 pieces of elastic ¼" wide, 8" long

Procedure: Draw around each foot on paper (about ½" larger than foot measures when weight is on it). Cut out. Trace patterns on wood. Saw around line with coping or jig saw. Sand edges. Nail 2½" blocks to toe end of shoes and smaller ones to heel ends. Tack center of ribbon on top of shoe at point between first and second toes. Tack ends under sole just in front of heel block. Tack ends of elastic to center sides of shoe so it will stretch around heel. (Adjust ribbon and elastic to fit.)

Time required to make: 2 to 3 hours

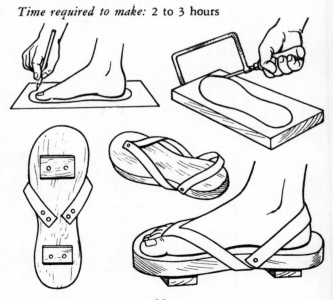

BEAN JEWELRY

Materials: Navy beans (about 300), 2 yd. waxed thread, needle, nail polish, 2 wooden beads about ⅜" diameter

Procedure: Soak beans overnight in water, drain and dry. Thread needle with waxed thread and tie knot about 2" from one end. String beans through center onto thread. When beans are strung to length of five feet, hang string from pole or line so that beans will not touch any object. With nail polish (any color desired) lightly coat each bean, beginning at top. Let dry. When beans are thoroughly dry, add wooden bead (also painted with nail polish) to each end. (Untie knot at knotted 'end, slip bead on thread and retie knot as close to bead as possible.) Wind beads around neck and tie in latest fashion.

Time required to make: 2 hours

91

SHOE BOX BAROMETER

Materials: 11" gut violin D string, 1 metal weight (medium-size fishing sinker or medium iron nut), 5" disc of heavy cardboard or light plywood with small hole in exact center, 1 large shoe box with lid, scissors, pencil, sealing wax, glue, Scotch tape, spray enamel, crayons, 1 plain index card, strips of light cardboard in these sizes: 3" x 18", 4½" x 13", two 4" x 2" strips

Procedure: Tie weight to end of gut string and soak string for short time in water. Hang to dry over a warm place. Note direction of twist as it dries. If it turns to the right while drying the sad duck will be attached to the left side of disc and vice versa. The sad duck should appear in warm weather and the glad duck in wet weather. Put string through hole in disc and put a drop of sealing wax in hole to attach disc firmly to string.

Trace pattern of ducks on index card and cut out, color

glad duck

sad duck

a

92

and attach to disc on opposites sides (see sketch b). Be sure the ducks are attached to the proper sides firmly with Scotch tape. Cut one end off the shoe box lid. Cut 3" out of one end of the bottom of the shoe box. Measure 3" above first cut area, draw doors as indicated in sketch c and cut out. Push end of violin string through hole in uncut end of box, about ½" from former bottom side. Tie string firmly. The disc should be flush with the bottom of the doors but should not rub any surface. Adjustments will probably have to be made in order to balance and adjust to weather properly.

Use 4½" x 13" strip for roof. Fold in half and attach with the 2" x 4" strips that have been folded in half like a hinge. Glue to top of box (see sketch d). Put lid on back of box with cut end at the bottom. Put 3" x 18" strip around front of box to conceal disc. Glue lid and front strip in place. Carefully spray entire house with bright enamel. Avoid spraying the disc, animals or gut string. Adjust as needed and use.

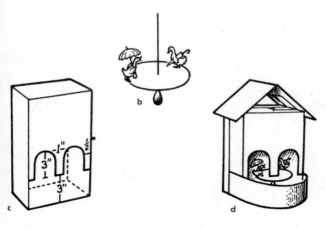

Time required to make: 1½ to 2 hours

BATH SALTS

Materials: 1 cup Epsom salts, 6 drops glycerin, 3 drops oil of roses, cake or vegetable coloring, wax paper, jars or fancy bottles

Procedure: The following recipe will make about one cup of bath salts. For the best results, make only one cup at a time. Empty one cup of Epsom salts on wax paper. Add six drops of glycerin and three drops of oil of roses. (Cologne may be substituted, using six drops.) Mix with fingers until well blended. Add a few drops of cake or vegetable coloring, delicately tinting the salts. Dry. Put in jars or fancy bottles. If layers of colors are desired, use widemouthed jar and insert wax paper perpendicularly in jar. Pour the salts in, then remove papers gently. If you wish, you may decorate jar top with paint, jewels or felt cutouts.

Time required to make: 20 to 30 minutes

BARK PICTURES

Materials: Different kinds of bark, moss, and other dry woodland materials, Wilhold glue, piece of white cardboard 10" x 12" or similar size, poster paint, brush, pencil, spray shellac

Procedure: Sketch desired scene on cardboard. Allow ½" margin all around cardboard for framing. Allow plenty of foreground space for gluing on bark, twigs, etc. Paint background with poster paints. (See sketch a.) Lay pieces of bark in foreground and glue in place. Create a woodland scene. (See sketch b.) (A very clever mosaic can be done with bark also.) Spray finished scene with shellac. Frame in regular frame or make one from heavy paper, cardboard or wood.

Time required to make: 40 to 60 minutes

a

b

COIN PURSE

Materials: Lightweight calf or goat skin leather 9"
square, leather tools, one yard plastic lacing, leather punch,
scissors, lacing needle

Procedure: Cut leather as in sketch a. With smooth side
up, fold up along dotted lines. To make firm crease, dampen leather slightly and press. Fold smooth sides back,
diagonally, as indicated in sketch b. Be sure that fold is
from corner to corner. Leather may be tooled on shaded
area. Punch holes along adjacent cut edges being careful
to space them evenly. Cut lacing into 9" lengths and lace

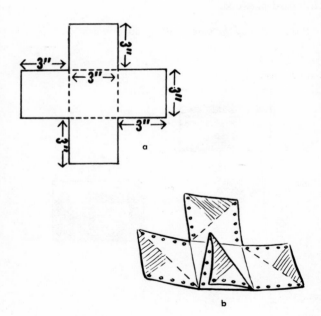

a

b

down each side from top to bottom, using both ends in an over and under manner (sketch c). Fasten lacing ends at

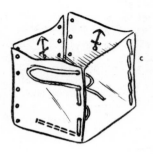

bottom on inside of purse. Fold sides down along diagonal creases to make purse flat (sketch d).

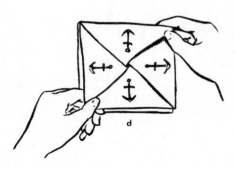

Time required to make: 60 minutes

COWL

Materials: 24" square of soft material (color and fabric depend upon when cowl will be worn), 24" square of contrasting color, needle, pins, thread, pinking shears

For beach wear these cowls may be made of terry cloth with seersucker or gingham lining. Use light cottons for summer, woolens and flannels for winter, silk jersey or taffeta for evenings.

Procedure: Enlarge hood and tie patterns according to dimensions given. Fold material in half. Place hood pattern on cloth as noted and cut out hood. Cut second hood (lining) from contrasting color following same directions. Cut two ties of each color from remaining material. (Patterns allow for ½" seams.)

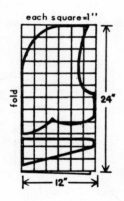

each square=1''

fold

24"

12"

Stitch around top of outer hood, starting at folded edge; then stitch around top of second hood. Place 2 ties together (one each color with right sides facing) and stitch together, leaving opening on smallest straight side. Turn right side out. Stitch second tie. Press both ties.

Place two hoods together, right sides facing, and match center top seams and edges. Baste or pin together. Stitch from *A* around top to *B*. Keep work wrong side out, insert one tie inside of hood to fit into (*A*) seam and stitch. Insert other tie into hood to fit (*B*) section and stitch.

Turn hood right side out. Turn bottom edges in and sew them together with small stitches. Or finish with binding tape. Press and turn cuff back on top. The hood is reversible.

Instead of tie, the two front seams can be stitched and buttons, snaps or hooks sewn on for fastening. Or fasten with a large safety pin.

Time required to make: **1½ to 2 hours**

FOIL CRAFT SCULPTURED PICTURE

Materials: Several foil pie plates or other foil containers, scissors, long-nosed pliers, copper wire, pencil, wire clothes hanger, spray can of paint

Procedure: Draw flowers, leaves, blossoms and other parts of picture on smooth parts of foil containers and cut the parts out (sketch a). Shape the coat hanger to desired form (sketch b). To make flowers, twist a length of copper wire around pencil and then remove pencil. Push one end of twist through center of flower and attach to coat hanger by twisting the wire around the coat hanger with pliers (sketch c). Bend petals to natural shape. To attach leaves, lay them alongside the copper wire and twist one end of leaf firmly around wire with pliers. Bend to shape. Squeeze until leaf is firmly placed (sketch d).

Work out your own ideas in design and flower shapes. When finished spray with paint and lay aside to dry. Use hook to hang or cut the hook off just above the twist and hook the bottom of the twist over a nail or picture hanger to hang it on the wall (sketch e).

Time required to make: 1 to 1½ hours

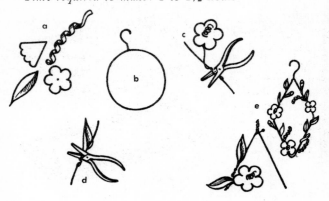

100

SERVING TRAYS

Materials: Pieces of plywood, ¼" to ¾" thick, and about 7" x 15" or 10" x 17"; scraps of wood for handles; molding; small finishing nails; hammer; screws; screwdriver; glue; coping saw; sandpaper; pencil; paper; paint or lacquer; brush

Procedure: Design type of tray you wish to make. Lap trays are usually 7" x 15" while all-purpose trays are approximately 16" in diameter for round trays and 10" x 17" for oblong trays. Smooth edges of board with sandpaper.

Make pattern on paper for type of handles you wish to have on tray. See sketch a for suggestions. Trace and cut handles from wood with coping saw. Sandpaper carefully. (Metal and plastic handles can be obtained from hardware store.) Handles can be glued, nailed or screwed to tray directly or to a piece of beveled molding which in turn can be nailed to tray. Nail or glue strips of molding along sides of tray. Spray or paint the tray as desired.

Time required to make: 1½ hours

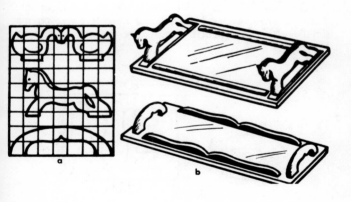

SCUFFS

Materials: Select a heavy plastic, imitation leather or quilted plastic 14"x22" for size 7 shoe (approximate size depends on shoe size); sponge rubber or cotton; binding tape matching material; 16" of 1"-wide elastic; needle; heavy thread

Procedure: Trace around your right foot and add ½" border around outside of foot tracing. Cut out and use for sole pattern. To make top of scuff, trace around front half

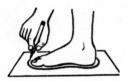

of foot. Add ¾" border around outside of tracing. Cut away a section of this top, using the dimensions on the pattern for a guide (see sketch).

Fold material in half (11"x14") and trace a right sole. Turn pattern over for left foot and trace left sole on material with colored pencil. Trace right top and reverse for left top of scuff.

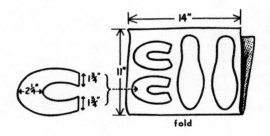

Insert layer of sponge padding or foam rubber (or several layers of cotton), between folds of material. Fasten with paper clips or pins. Now cut out soles and tops ¼" outside stitching line. Stitch around soles and tops with strong thread. If material tears in stitching, sew by hand, whipping edges together with heavy thread. If cotton padding is used, stitch squares as in quilting. Fit right top on right sole and stitch edges together. Fit and stitch left scuff. Stitch a 4" length of wide elastic to outside end of top piece for heel on each scuff. Decorate with plastic flowers or ruffles if desired. Bind sole edges with binding tape or Mystik Tape. Quilted terry cloth may be used for tops of scuffs.

Time required to make: 2 to 3 hours

"MY FIND" BOOKENDS

Materials: Plaster of Paris, interesting pieces of rock, bark, pine cones, or driftwood or other natural items (enough for even distribution on both book ends); two 18" x 18" sheets of aluminum foil, 2 strips of light cardboard 3" x 24", Scotch tape, water, tempera if desired

Procedure: Make molds for book ends by folding each cardboard strip 6" from one end and 6" from other end. Bring the two ends together and overlap as in sketch a. Tape ends together. Lay each cardboard mold on 1 sheet of foil. Bring sides of foil up over top of mold sides and squeeze to mold shape. (See sketch b.) Be careful not to puncture or wrinkle foil on bottom of mold. Do not put foil more than 1" down the inside of mold.

Pour plaster mixed to a very creamy consistency equally into the 2 molds. As it begins to set put nature objects into the mold near the flat side so the object will help support the books. (See sketch c.) If desired, a little tempera paint can be mixed into the plaster before pouring to color the book ends. When the plaster has hardened thoroughly, remove the molds.

Time required to make: 40 to 50 minutes

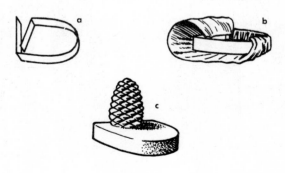

END TABLE

Materials: Three boards 12", 16", 20" long and 8" wide; four 2" strips, each 24" long; hammer; shellac; file or sandpaper; saw; nails

Procedure: Saw off top and bottom of each leg at slight angle so that ends are parallel (sketch a). Smooth all pieces, especially the corners, with sandpaper. Nail legs to top shelf first so that end of leg is even with top of table. Nail middle shelf about halfway down and lowest shelf near bottom of legs (sketch b). Shellac and allow to dry.

Alternate Suggestion: Make end table with two shelves, using the same directions, but use only two boards instead of three (sketch c). Size of boards may be varied.

Time required to make: 60 minutes

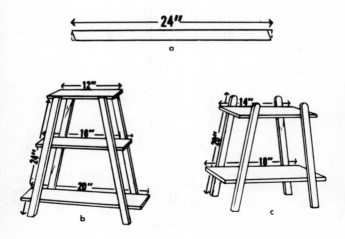

SECRET COMPARTMENT WALLET

Materials: Heavy plastic or imitation leather 9″x9¾″
(½ yd. of 54″ material makes 10 wallets); yarn, waxed
cord or lacing for binding; awl; crochet hook; cardboard;
scissors; paper clips

Procedure: Enlarge pattern on cardboard according to
dimensions given in sketch, and cut out. Trace pattern on
back of imitation leather and cut out. Fold down section

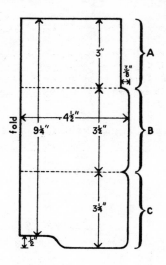

A and fold up section *C*. Secure along folds with paper
clips. Piece *A* is cut smaller than *B* and *C* so it will fit down
inside to form secret compartment. Be careful not to catch
edges of *A* in stitching.

Finish edges of wallet with lacing or cord. Hold wallet
with inside facing you. Begin work on center of left side.
Punch a hole with awl ¼″ from edge. Draw binding ma-

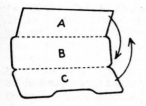 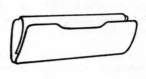

terial through hole with hook. Slip short end of cord down inside of wallet. Punch holes as you work. Work along edges in blanket stitch. Keep stitches taut, but do not pucker material. Holes for the stitches should be ¼" from edge and about 3/16" apart. To finish stitching, interlock first and last stitches of cord and slip end inside wallet and knot with starting end.

If craft leader is familiar with leather work, he may instruct pupils in binding their wallets with a cordovan stitch or show them how to decorate the imitation leather.

Time required to make: About 2 hours

WORM PIN CUSHION

Materials: 3 styrofoam balls 2″ in diameter, enough rug or knitting yarn to completely cover balls (amount depends on thickness of yarn), 1 yard contrasting yarn or ribbon, 3 sequins (2 of the same color), 4 straight pins, scissors, ruler

Procedure: Cut yarn into 24″ lengths. Cut enough to cover the balls completely. Double the lengths and tie in center. Pin the tied end to a ball. Pull the yarn evenly around the ball and tie on other side with 12″ of contrasting ribbon or yarn in a bow. (See sketch a.) Place another ball next to tie and cover it evenly with yarn. This time tie yarn at the top of the second ball. (See sketch a.) Place third ball on top of second tie and draw yarn evenly around it. Tie the yarn on top with last piece of ribbon or yarn. (See sketch a.) Trim left-over yarn into "butch hair cut" for worm. Place sequins for eyes and nose. (See sketch b.) If desired, cut a little from bottom of first 2 balls to make worm balance easier. Pins and needles can be pushed into worm's back.

Time required to make: 20 to 30 minutes

MEMO HOLDER

Materials: Cardboard tube 5" long and 1½" in diameter, colored paper or paint, 15 feet copper wire (type used to tie cartons for mailing), clip clothespin, 2 gummed reinforcements or beads, sharp thick needle

Procedure: Cover inside and outside of tube with colored paper or paint for body.

Legs: Cut 2 strips of copper wire 4½ feet long. With needle, punch 2 holes 1" apart and ½" from end of tube. Insert wire through holes; bring ends together outside tube and twist wire as close to tube as possible. Wind each wire tightly around broomstick. Remove broomstick. Repeat process for legs at other end.

Tail: Punch hole in body above one set of legs. Insert 12" wire through hole and out end of tube; fasten end close to body. Wind wire around pencil to make tail.

Neck and head: Punch a hole in body above front legs. Insert a 5-foot wire through the two front leg holes and fasten the end inside tube. Draw long end of wire through hole above legs and wind around broomstick. Cover clip clothespin with colored paper or paint. Add gummed reinforcements (or beads) for eyes. Fasten clothespin at end of neck coil. Clip memo in "mouth" of clothespin.

Time required to make: 60 minutes

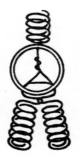

COAT HANGER PICTURE FRAME

Materials: 4 wooden coat hangers with metal carefully removed, sandpaper, enamel or varnish, paintbrush, glue or hammer and nails, ready-mixed moist gesso (from hobby shop or art supply store), brush, fancy thumbtacks (optional), picture, cardboard from tablet backs, adhesive tape, yarn or string

Procedure: Glue, or carefully nail, the four wooden hanger frames as shown in sketch a. Enamel in color desired or decorate with gesso. Brush gesso on wood and then make design with a comb. Or, stipple gesso with brush. If you wish, simply varnish the wooden hangers and decorate with fancy thumbtacks. (See sketch b.) When frame is completely dry, cut out a cardboard backing for picture and trim to fit frame. Mount picture carefully and glue mounted picture to frame as shown in sketch c. Use adhesive tape and a piece of colored string or yarn for a hanger. Attach as shown in sketch d.

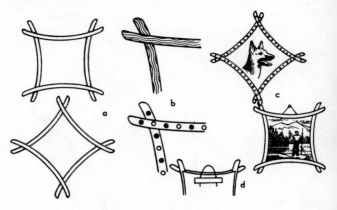

Time required to make: 1 to 2 hours

PLASTIC PAPERWEIGHT

Materials: Plexiglas or other clear plastic block 1¾" x
1¾" x 2½", power saw for cutting to size, brace and 3/16"
bit or power drill with same size bit, sandpaper, felt 2½" x
1¾", glue, scissors

Procedure: Cut block of plastic to size. Sand all rough
edges until smooth. Stand block so clear sides are at the
side, not top and bottom. With brace and bit or power
drill, drill holes into bottom of block at several angles. Be
careful not to go through the side of block or all the way
through. Drill only the bottom side. After drilling, cover
bottom with felt.

Time required to make: 1 hour

RECIPES

SOAPSUDS PAINT

> 1 cup any powder detergent
> 4 tbs. liquid starch

Mix detergent and starch and beat with a rotary beater until mixture is like frosting. If colored paint is desired, add powder paint or a drop of vegetable coloring.

Paint will last about one day so should be made on the day to be used. If the mixture becomes thick, add a little starch and beat it with a spoon. This recipe will provide paint for 8 to 10 children.

PASTE

> 1 cup sugar   1 qt. warm water
> 1 cup flour   1 tsp. powdered alum
>   Few drops oil of cloves

Mix dry ingredients in top of double boiler. Add water

slowly, stirring continuously. Cook until clear, and a little longer. Remove from fire, add oil of cloves, mixing thoroughly. Cool. Place in bottles or jars. Cover. Will keep for several months if carefully prepared. This recipe makes one quart.

SALT CLAY

Many interesting projects can be made from salt clay. It is easy to use, simple to prepare and washes off hands easily. Encourage originality. Trace the outline of object to be made on heavy cardboard. Draw in whatever design is desired beyond section where clay is to be applied. Shellac cardboard to keep it from absorbing the clay moisture. Mold clay on cardboard to show desired features. Allow time to dry—usually two days. Then if coloring was not mixed into clay, paint with water colors.

1 cup salt	1 cup water
2 cups flour	Vegetable coloring
Oil of cloves or oil of wintergreen, several drops	

Mix salt and flour with water to consistency of heavy dough. Add oil of cloves or oil of wintergreen, mixing thoroughly. This acts as a preservative. Vegetable coloring can be kneaded into clay, or objects can be made first, then colored with water colors. This recipe makes about 12 pictures or small objects.

(To help the salt clay retain its shape better, make the dough a little more moist and then cook over low heat and stir until it is very thick.)

PAPIER-MACHE

Papier-mache craft can be very exciting and rewarding. You can make plaques, relief pictures, maps and models.

1 newspaper (16 to 20 sheets)	Hot water
1 tsp. powdered alum	1 pt. paste
Optional—add starch or flour	

Tear newspaper into small pieces and soak overnight in a pail of hot water. Shred between fingers until it is a pulpy mass. Pour off water or strain through a cloth. Add alum to paste and mix thoroughly with pulp. Add enough starch or flour, if desired, to make pulp the consistency of clay. Apply as desired to make a design on wood, cardboard, model, etc.

This recipe will make about $\frac{1}{2}$ pail of papier-mache which is enough to make approximately 12 maps or flat objects. Allow two or three days for object to dry.

If you plan to cover an entire object, several layers of papier-mache may be needed. Paint with poster paints when dry. Shellac for permanence.

HINTS

PLASTER CASTING

Many lovely and useful articles can be made from plaster of Paris, molding plaster or patching plaster. All can be used the same way so shop around and purchase whichever is the cheapest.

Figurine, animal and motto molds are available for making objects to correlate with Bible lessons. Plaques and pins can be made practically expense free by all ages. The plaster also can be carved to make attractive pictures. Try these ways of using plaster and see what fun it is.

Nearly all plaster includes directions. For casting purposes, mix plaster with water until the consistency is that of a thick batter. Be very sparing when adding water! Remember, plaster hardens quickly and once it sets, it's set!

1. Molded plaster

One place where you may obtain figurine, animal or plaque molds is: Bersted's Hobby Craft, Inc., Monmouth, Illinois. Write for an illustrated catalog.

Wash molds in cold water and shake out. Inside should be damp. Prepare plaster and spoon it into mold. Squeeze out air bubbles and allow plaster to set (about 12 to 20 minutes). Gently peel mold—slowly—and trim off rough edges. Allow to dry completely, then paint with water colors or poster paints.

2. Plaster gifts

Obtain a supply of pictures, safety pins, adhesive tape, small fluted paper plates, milk cartons, colorless fingernail polish, hairpins, spoons, rubber furniture cups, Vaseline, plaster, bowl. (One two-pound package of plaster will make about 36 pins and about 24 plaques.)

Select the designs desired for pins or plaques from greeting cards. Prepare molds by cutting milk cartons down to within 1" of the bottom, or by greasing spoons, plates or rubber furniture cups lightly with Vaseline. Place picture or design face down in each mold and mark edge of mold where the top of pin or plaque is. Mix plaster with water until it is a thick pouring consistency. Pour into molds and set in sun.

To make a plaque, insert a hairpin in top of plaque for hanger when the plaster begins to "set." (Yarn or paper clips will also do. To make a pin, insert an open safety pin in plaster, being careful not to let the head fall in too deeply. Place a piece of adhesive tape across safety pin to prevent it from breaking out.

When plaster is hard, ease plaque or pin from mold. Cardboard and rubber molds are best since they are flexible. Use emery board to smooth off ends; cover with colorless fingernail polish. If twin pins are desired, fasten together with a length of gold or silver chain, available at the ten cent stores.

3. Carving in plaster

Use the above method for molding a plaque in a paper plate. While plaster is damp and still in mold, outline a design with an orange stick. As plaque dries, carve out the design in relief with orange stick or knife. Paint when dry.

HELPFUL HINTS for Patterns

There are patterns in this book to be prepared for use. You will also find designs elsewhere which you will want to use. The following hints will help you.

Tracing

Use tracing or tissue paper.

1. With small pieces of masking tape, fasten tracing paper lightly to page of book or on item to be traced. Trace around outline with sharp pencil.

2. To transfer tracing onto another surface, turn tracing paper over and cover back with pencil scribbles by using side of pencil lead.

3. With masking tape, anchor tracing on top of cloth or paper on which you wish to transfer design. Then go over lines of design with pencil. Remove tracing paper and design is transferred.

Enlarging and Reducing Patterns

To make the design twice as large:

1. On tracing paper, mark off every ½" lengthwise and crosswise. Draw in ½" squares with pencil and ruler.

2. Place this sheet over design and trace outline.

3. Make a copy sheet out of a second piece of tracing paper by ruling it off in 1" squares.

4. Study lines of design on the first tracing paper, then draw them in corresponding positions on the copy sheet.

To make the design half size:

1. Reverse method above.

2. Mark off first tracing sheet with ½" squares and copy sheet with ¼" squares.

When design is right size, transfer to material as instructed under "Tracing."

HOW TO CUT GLASS

Glass can be easily cut for use in making handcraft projects. Obtain a good glass cutter from a hardware store, a metal-edge ruler, a grease pencil, a piece of coarse grinding stone such as is used to sharpen tools.

Glass should be cut by adults for the younger child but teenagers can cut their own if they are properly shown how to do it. Care should be taken to avoid cuts and unplanned breakage.

1. Measure and mark on glass with grease pencil the portions you wish to cut.

2. Hold a ruler firmly against glass on cutting line and press heavily with glass cutter as you pull or push it along the edge of the ruler.

3. Place glass so the cutting line is on the edge of a table. Gently press the overhanging section until the glass breaks. Smooth all the edges gently with the grinding stone. For young children, the edges may be bound with Scotch tape to insure against accidental cuts.